The Fantastic Jungles of Henri Rousseau

Written by MICHELLE MARKEL

Illustrated by AMANDA HALL

Eerdmans Books for Young Readers

Grand Rapids, Michigan • Cambridge, U.K.

Text © 2012 Michelle Markel
Illustrations © 2012 Amanda Hall

Published in 2012 by Eerdmans Books for Young Readers,
an imprint of Wm. B. Eerdmans Publishing Co.
2140 Oak Industrial Dr. NE
Grand Rapids, Michigan 49505
P.O. Box 163, Cambridge CB3 9PU U.K.

www.eerdmans.com/youngreaders

Manufactured at Tien Wah Press in Malaysia

15 16 17 18   9 8 7 6 5 4

Library of Congress Cataloging-in-Publication Data

Markel, Michelle.
The fantastic jungles of Henri Rousseau / by Michelle Markel ; illustrated by Amanda Hall.
p. cm.
ISBN 978-0-8028-5364-6 (alk. paper)
1. Rousseau, Henri, 1844-1910 — Juvenile literature. 2. Painters — France — Biography — Juvenile literature.
I. Rousseau, Henri, 1844-1910. II. Hall, Amanda. III. Title.
ND553.R67M37 2012
759.4 — dc23
2011035838

The illustrations were rendered in watercolor and acrylics.
The display type was set in French Script STD.
The text type was set in Adobe Garamond Pro.

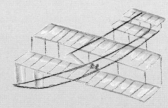

FSC
www.fsc.org
MIX
Paper from
responsible sources
FSC® C012700

To my mother, for her love and encouragement.
— *M M*

In memory of my father, the artist John Hall.
— *A.H.*

Henri Rousseau wants to be an artist.
Not a single person has ever told him he is talented.
He's a toll collector.
He's forty years old.

But he buys some canvas, paint, and brushes,
and starts painting anyway.

Why? Because he loves nature. Because when he strolls through the parks of Paris, it's like the flowers open their hearts, the trees spread their arms, and the sun is a blushing ruby, all for him.

Henri can't afford art lessons, so he has to be his own teacher.
He goes to the Louvre and examines the satiny
paintings of his favorite artists.

To learn about anatomy, he studies photographs and illustrations from postcards, magazines, and catalogues.

One day Henri reads about a big art exhibition. He puts his canvases in a handcart and wheels them to the building where the show will be held. He's forty-one years old, and this is the very first time he'll display his work! He can hardly wait to hear what the experts will say.

Mean things. That's what most of them write. But Henri snips out the articles anyway, and pastes them in a scrapbook.

Henri walks around the city, gathering ideas for his pictures. He goes to the World's Fair, where a man named Eiffel has built a latticed tower of metal rising several hundred feet into the air.

What thrills Henri most are the fair's exhibits of villages from distant lands. They remind him of adventure stories he loved when he was a boy.

Days later, Henri can still picture the plants and animals from faraway places. He holds his paintbrush to the canvas. A tiger crawls out. Lightning strikes, and wind whips the jungle grass.

Sometimes Henri is so startled by what he paints that he has to open the window to let in some air.

Every year Henri goes back to the art exhibition to show new paintings.
He fusses over the canvases and retouches them until the last minute.

And every year the art experts make fun of him. They say it looks like he
closed his eyes and painted with his feet.

Henri keeps painting and learning. In the fall he collects
leaves from the cemetery to sketch. He spends
hours drawing at the Jardin des Plantes,
where — oh happiness! — a gardener
sneaks him into the hothouses.

Towering palms spread their giant fans; tropical plants fruit
and flower into garlands, rockets, and rosettes of color.

When Henri walks through the glass doorway,
it's as though he enters into a dream. It's like
he is someone else completely.

One day Henri paints a still desert night, bathed in moon glow. He sees a gypsy sleeping. A lion creeps up, but does no harm.

Once again he takes his work to the art show. This time, perhaps, he'll please the experts. His pulse races.

The experts say he paints like a child. "If you want to have a good laugh," one of them writes, "go see the paintings by Henri Rousseau."

By now Henri is used to the nasty critics. He knows his shapes are simpler and flatter than everyone else's, but he thinks that makes them lovely. He spends all he earns on art supplies, and pays for his bread and coal with landscapes and portraits. In the afternoon he takes off his frayed smock and gives music lessons. His home is a shabby little studio, where one pot of stew must last the whole week. But every morning he wakes up and smiles at his pictures.

Henri turns sixty-one years old. Because of
his poverty, he'll never travel to a real jungle.
It doesn't matter — he sees one before him,
clear as day. For weeks he fills in his jungle,
tenderly shaping every fern, every frond,
every blade and leaf. As always, when
Henri finishes the painting, he takes it
to the exhibition.

Many experts mock him. One says only
cavemen would be impressed by his art.

But this time several artists disagree.

The artists are much younger than Rousseau
and are already well known. They befriend him.

And whenever Henri has money to spare, and stages a
concert in his little studio, all the artists come. Along with
the grocer, locksmith, and other folks from the neighborhood,
they listen to Henri's students and friends play their musical instruments.
Henri gives the shiniest, reddest apples to the children.

One night a well-known artist named Picasso throws a banquet for Henri. The old man sits upon a makeshift throne. Poets recite poems for him. Guests sing songs and make speeches. Henri plays his little violin, and people dance to the music. His heart floats like a hot-air balloon above the fields.

Toward the end of his life Henri makes a remarkable painting called "The Dream," his biggest ever. As he does every year, he displays it at the exhibition and anxiously awaits the reviews.

A famous poet writes, "I don't think anyone will laugh this year."

Fcw people do.

A hundred years later, the flowers still blossom, the monkeys still frolic, and the snakes keep slithering through Henri's hot jungles. His paintings now hang in museums all over the world. And do you think experts call them "foolish," "clumsy," or "monstrous"? *Mais non!* They call them works of art.
> By an old man,
> by a onetime toll collector,
> by one of the most gifted self-taught artists in history:
> *Henri Rousseau*

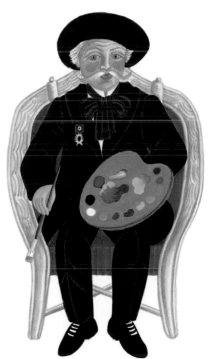

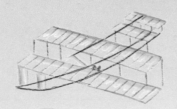

Author's Note:

Naïve: adjective 1. Lacking experience, wisdom, or judgment. 2. (of art or an artist) produced in or adopting a simple, childlike style which deliberately rejects sophisticated techniques. Origin: French, from Latin nativus "native, natural"

Henri Rousseau was the first "naïve" artist to be recognized as a great master. Born in 1844 to a family of modest means living in a French market town, he later moved to Paris. It was not until he was in his forties, employed as a toll collector, that he took up painting. His nickname was *"Le Douanier"* (or "customs officer"). In 1885 Rousseau tried to exhibit his art at the official Salon run by the Ministry of Painting and Sculpture, but was refused. A year later he showed his paintings at the Salon des Indépendants, which did not have judges or juries. He was ridiculed year after year, but gradually developed a following. Avant-garde artists and writers such as Picasso, Delaunay, Jarry, and Apollinaire admired his innocence and charm.

Rousseau is best known for the paintings he made of jungles. As he never actually left Paris, the tropical imagery came solely from his imagination and from his visits to the zoo and botanical gardens. He told a journalist, "I don't know if you're like me . . . but when I go into the glass houses and I see the strange plants of exotic lands, it seems to me that I enter into a dream. I feel that I'm somebody else completely."

Although in the late 1800s he received commissions for paintings and attention from art dealers and collectors, Rousseau never enjoyed financial success. He died of gangrene in 1910 at a Paris hospital and was buried in a pauper's grave. Shortly afterward, his work received the worldwide recognition it deserved. Many of his techniques influenced younger generations of artists.

— M. M.

Illustrator's Note:

I first saw Henri Rousseau's paintings when I was sixteen. It was as though someone had turned on a light in my head, a light that shone on something I recognized or remembered. His images still have the same power to inspire me today. I also found Michelle Markel's poignant telling of his story very moving, so I was delighted to be chosen to illustrate this book.

Before getting down to work, I made a special trip to Paris to research many of the places that are featured in the book. In addition to studying pictures from the era, I read about Henri's life and the famous people he knew. It was fascinating to get to know more about him through these explorations.

Instead of my usual pencil crayon and watercolor technique, I used both watercolor and acrylics for the illustrations, as I wanted to get close to the feel of Rousseau's own paintings. I decided to break the rules of scale and perspective to reflect his unusual way of seeing the world. For some of the illustrations, I drew inspiration from his actual paintings, altering them playfully to help tell the story.

Illustrating this book has been a real labor of love for me. I hope Henri would have liked it, and I do hope you enjoy it too.

— A. H.

Some of the spreads in this book depict famous historical figures whom Rousseau knew during his life.
Use this key to discover who they were.

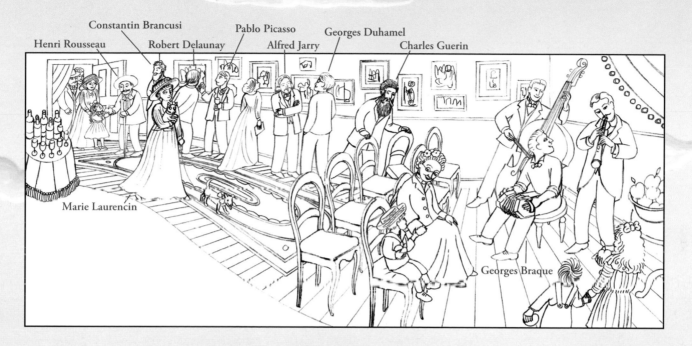

Henri Rousseau · Constantin Brancusi · Robert Delaunay · Pablo Picasso · Alfred Jarry · Georges Duhamel · Charles Guerin

Marie Laurencin

Georges Braque

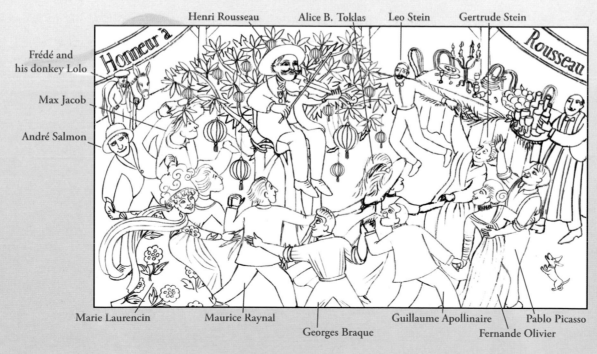

Henri Rousseau · Alice B. Toklas · Leo Stein · Gertrude Stein

Frédé and his donkey Lolo

Max Jacob

André Salmon

Honneur à

Rousseau

Marie Laurencin · Maurice Raynal · Georges Braque · Guillaume Apollinaire · Fernande Olivier · Pablo Picasso